Stock Trading for Beginners:

How to Start

Table of Contents

Introduction 5
Chapter 1: What are Stocks? 7
Chapter 2: Who Participates in the Stock Market? 11
Chapter 3: Order Types of the Market 15
Chapter 4: Let's Get Started 22
Chapter 5: What Kind of Trader Do I Want To Be? 30
Chapter 6: Getting Started With Less Money 33
Chapter 7: Putting It All Together 40
Conclusion 43

© Copyright 2018 by _____ - All rights reserved.

The following eBook is reproduced below with the goal of providing information that is as accurate and reliable as possible. Regardless, purchasing this eBook can be seen as consent to the fact that both the publisher and the author of this book are in no way experts on the topics discussed within and that any recommendations or suggestions that are made herein are for entertainment purposes only. Professionals should be consulted as needed prior to undertaking any of the action endorsed herein.

This declaration is deemed fair and valid by both the American Bar Association and the Committee of Publishers Association and is legally binding throughout the United States.

Furthermore, the transmission, duplication, or reproduction of any of the following work including specific information will be considered an illegal act irrespective of if it is done electronically or in print. This extends to creating a secondary or tertiary copy of the work or a recorded copy and is only allowed with the express written consent from the Publisher. All additional right reserved.

The information in the following pages is broadly considered a truthful and accurate account of facts and as such, any inattention, use, or misuse of the information in question by the reader will render any resulting actions solely under their purview. There are no scenarios in which the publisher or the original author of this work can be in any fashion deemed liable for any hardship or damages that may befall them after undertaking information described herein.

Additionally, the information in the following pages is intended only for informational purposes and should thus be thought of as universal. As befitting its nature, it is presented without assurance regarding its prolonged validity or interim quality. Trademarks that are mentioned are done without written consent and can in no way be considered an endorsement from the trademark holder.

Introduction

Congratulations on downloading *Stock Trading for Beginners: How to Start,* and thank you for doing so. When you start thinking about stock trading and researching the information that is out there, you can get quite overwhelmed. The world is evolving fast and just as so, so are the stocks! You don't want to jump in without a good idea of what you are getting into. Downloading this book is taking the first step into getting into the trades. This is the easy part. However, you will find information that can help you develop a well-thought-out plan and put it into action right away without breaking your bank account.

With that said, stock trading can be quite confusing if you don't have a general understanding of what stocks are. When you start researching it online, the information can get overwhelming. The following chapters will explain who uses the stock market besides the investors, the difference between stockholders and bondholders, and what common stock is compared to preferred stock and bonds. We will discuss what owning stock in a company means and why companies sell stock. It's important to know the difference in the types of traders and how it applies to you and your financial goals.

There are risks that you need to be aware of as well as certain rules to keep in mind in order to be successful. Here, we will go into detail and break it down into simple steps, remind you of things to watch out, for and help you get the best bang for your buck! Worried that you can't afford to purchase stock? That's okay! You don't have to be a millionaire to purchase and trade stock. We will also cover how to begin buying and trading stock with little money. You will learn everything from how to use your employer to invest to investing with the United States government.

There are several different books on this subject on the market, so thank you for choosing this one! Every effort was made to ensure that this eBook is full of as much useful information as possible. Please enjoy!

Chapter 1: What are Stocks?

Getting started into stock trading can be quite confusing unless you know what exactly stocks are and its different types. Stocks are considered investments. When a person purchases stock from a company, they are called shareholders. Once you become a shareholder of a company, you now own a share. A share is issued by the corporation. This does not mean you own part of the company; that belongs to the corporation. You simply own a share of the company's profits.

The idea of stocks is for the companies to sell them to investors to raise more money to grow the business. In turn, that generates more revenue or income for the business. With more revenue, the value increases along with company profits. Companies that are public usually go through a stock exchange market to sell their stocks.

When purchasing stocks in a company, you always hope that the value will increase. Most people tend to think that stocks only raise in value due to capital appreciation. That's not necessarily true. Stocks sometimes will pay dividends, which is cash you collect for being the owner. However, that doesn't always happen. Being down on your luck happens to everyone, even businesses. Sometimes business isn't booming as usual due to several different reasons, or even worse, the company goes out of business. When this happens, the investor can lose some, if not all, of his investment in that company. Stock prices change frequently all throughout the day, so things can be increasing one minute and on a decline the next minute. That's why it is important to spread your investments around into different companies, not just focusing on one company.

Owning a stock isn't just purchasing through a stock market exchange. In fact, there are a lot of people that own stock through their jobs with a 401(k) and don't even realize it. Most of the employer retirement plans invest in mutual funds. Money is pooled together on behalf of investors and the mutual fund then invests in several different types of companies, in different locations, and more. It's basically the wholesale club of the stock market world.

Now that we have a basic idea of what stocks are, let's explain the two common types of stocks: common stock and preferred stock.

- **Common stock.** The name itself is self-explanatory. This is the most common type of stock that investors own. It is a form of equity and security. This type of stock not only lets you share in the company's profits but also earns you the right to vote. No, not in the presidential election! You still need to register for that. You earn the right to vote on different issues such as voting on members for the board of directors, splitting of stocks, and other objectives amongst the corporation. The issues shareholders can vote on also vary by corporation. However, sometimes, common stock can be split into voting and non-voting classes. You would need to check on the voting rights to the corporation that you invested common stock in.

While common stock may be the most common type of stock. When it comes to compensation if a company goes bankrupt, common stock shareholders are at the bottom of the totem pole. In other words, everyone gets compensated before common stock shareholders. The money that remains after bondholders, employees, other creditors, and preferred stockholders are compensated is then distributed to the common stock investors. Literally, they are the last investor to be compensated! It is not uncommon for common stock investors to receive zero compensation after a company files for bankruptcy.

- **Preferred stock.** This type of stock ranks higher than common stock. It serves as both an equity and instrument of debt. It may or may not have a fixed liquidation value, but it does have a claim on the liquidation proceeds equal to its value. However, it is not at the top of the totem pole when it comes to compensation after bankruptcy either. Preferred stock may serve a higher ranking than common stock investors, but they still fall behind bondholders.

Common stock and preferred stock can both have claims to income in the aspect of capital appreciation. As with any company, when the value increases, so does the value of the equity, meaning shareholders receive a return on their investments. The amount of the return will vary between common stock investors and preferred stock investors. This is due to the different prices and rewards based on the different kinds of shares. However, on average, common shareholders have a higher return over preferred stock owners and even bondholders from increasing value of the stocks.

Just as shareholders can receive a return on their investment, they can also lose. As we mentioned earlier in the chapter, business can decrease for a company for several reasons. When business decreases, this, in turn, will decrease the value of the equity. When the value of the equity decreases this will reflect a loss on the investment and lower the value of shareholders claims to income.

- Bondholders differ from common stock and preferred stock owners. They have a higher sense of security because, in the event of liquidation or bankruptcy, a bondholder ranks the highest on the totem pole for compensation. A bondholder has a loan agreement (bond) between themselves (bondholder) and an issuer. The issuer usually being a company or the government. A bondholder is considered a lender, meaning the company sell their bond to be able to borrow said funds and repay. Interest is usually paid to the bondholder twice a year. Bonds can be bought and sold on a bond market and are typically considered to be a safer gamble when it comes to investing, over stock.

Now that we have a general understanding of the difference between shareholders and bondholders as well as the different types of stocks, we can move forward with learning to begin trading stocks! Knowing the risks and weighing the pros and cons are important when beginning in the stock market trading world. Making well-informed decisions on your financial future will probably fare better off than just jumping straight into it!

Chapter 2: Who Participates in the Stock Market?

The stock market is not just composed of the people who buy and sell stock. It is made up of several different bodies and agencies required and most regulated by the SEC. These agencies were put into place to ensure that things stay efficient and fair and maintain order within the market. Knowing who and what role they have will help you understand where you stand in the stock market and the different agencies that can help you.

Brokers

Brokers are sometimes referred to as dealers or broker-dealers. They bring the selling shareholders and the potential investing buyers together. In other words, they can sell their securities to a customer that is buying. They can also buy securities that a customer is trying to sell. Brokers oversee the trades, usually at a fee, between customers that are buying and selling securities. A broker can play as either role for one or the other but not for both.

Brokers usually are not very expensive. You just have to shop around! They have the best source of resources and tools to help you get the best investment from a vast variety of clients. However, be sure to research the broker you are considering. You want to make sure that they are licensed and have formal training on the matter. Knowledge is power, and it is not limited to just you. When just beginning into the trades, you want to choose a broker that has the knowledge and experience and one who has already established a relationship with their account holders.

Credit Agencies

Credit agencies are on the market to help you! Much like they do when you go and purchase a car at a dealership, credit agencies give their opinion or grades on a company or a security. The grade rating a company has will tell you if they are investment worthy or not. For example, grades of AAA can be assigned from a credit agency, meaning they are of investment grade. Credit ratings of, let's say, BB can mean that company or stock is not of investment grade. This can be useful information when deciding whether to buy or sell your security.

Clearing Agencies

Clearing agencies are considered Self-Reg Organizations. These agencies play the role of what I consider to be a school principal. They write the rules, make sure they are enforced, and discipline members when needed. There are two types of this agency: clearing corps and depositories.

- Clearing agencies such as NSCC or FICC look and compare transactions, clear, and prepare for settlement of those transactions. They often act as the "middle man."
- Depositories hold securities for its customers, as well as make transfers and keep ownership records up to date.

Investment Advisors

The name itself is self-explanatory. Investment advisors do just that, for a fee. The fee can either be a flat-rate set prior to agreement or set percentage of their clients' assets being managed. They can either be a person or a group of people that perform analysis of the stocks and provides the investor with the results and their opinions or, rather, recommendations. They have a special small amount of authority when it comes to their clients' investments. They can act on the behalf of the client and execute orders. However, this is not something they just automatically have in place when you enroll their services. Usually, during the enrolling process, you, the client, must formally provide discretionary authority to the advisor.

As a client, you have access to various customers, anywhere from small investors to big corporations. As long as you meet the minimum requirements set forth by the advisor, the size of your portfolio doesn't matter. Anyone can be a client to a financial advisor.

Transfer Agents

These agents maintain records of ownership, cancel securities, issue new ones, and pay out dividends when it is time. They are technically the "middleman" between the company issuing the security and the security holder, better known as the bank. They not only deal with canceling and issuing certificates and payouts but they also deal with the securities that have been lost or stolen and other problems that may arise from the investor. They also work with a registrar to ensure investment statements are mailed out monthly to the investors.

Not only do they work hard monthly to ensure their investors are kept up-to-date on their securities, but also, you also hear from them once a year when they send out annual reports that include the audited statements from the company and when the best time of year comes around, tax time. They send out the federal tax info to their investors.

Security Exchanges

These are also known as the stock market exchange. They are the markets where investors' stocks are bought and sold. Currently, there are 15 different exchange markets registered with the SEC. Examples being New York Stock Exchange and NASDAQ. Most of today's trades can be made through electronic trading, but there is also a facility that stockers and brokers can go and buy and sell securities. Security exchanges, whether at a facility or through online forums, are considered to be more like a twenty-four-hour auction. They are continuously going

The point of the stock exchange isn't just for buyers to buy stock and for sellers to sell it. The idea is also for the companies that put their stock on the market to have more opportunity for capital growth, through the vast diversity of the market exchange and the investors that utilize it.

ECNs

An ECN is an electronic trading system. In order for an investor to use an ECN, they must have an account that allows direct access trading. This system automatically matches up buy and sell orders for specific price amounts for its users. They are technically registered as broker-dealers with the SEC. They technically operate as an automated broker. The uniqueness of this option is that you are completely anonymous. Negotiations are generally done electronically.

Chapter 3: Order Types of the Market

Understanding the order types of the market is important to know. This will help you get the best bang for your buck and help you make the best decision for yourself and your stock. There are three main types: market, limit, and stop. However, there are many more that you need to know about that we will discuss in this chapter. Each serving their own unique purpose. Before deciding which type you will need to use, you must ask yourself two things:

1. Am I buying or selling my order?
2. What price am I willing to settle with? Higher, lower, or even?

Market Orders

Market orders are the easiest order types there are. They are primarily for getting orders executed sooner rather than later. It is suggested to only use this type of order if your concern is to get things done immediately as this is more focused on the now as opposed to the price.

To better understand this, stocks have an offer price and a bid price. Investors generally pay the offer price and then sell for the bidding price. A common mistake is to make a market order after hours. If a bad news story hits the air, the stock market does not necessarily react every time. You want to make sure before placing a market order that is necessary. Otherwise, you could lose instead of gain on your investment.

It is important to remember that, in this type of order, you have no control over the price that you receive. With the markets moving so fast all the time, the price you paid or the amount you received may be significantly different than the price that was last quoted before the order was entered. Just as the world moves fast, so does the prices of securities.

Limit Orders

Limit orders are for getting a security at a certain price or even better. While this type of order guarantees a specific price, it does not guarantee execution. This is helpful if you are buying as you can request that the price be below market value. If you are selling, you can specify the amount to be over market price. It is, more or less like buying a car or even selling one, depends on which side of the deal you are on.

For example, a sell-limit order can only be sold at a certain price or higher. However, a buy-limit order can be bought only at the limit price or lower. It is important to know that both of these orders can have additional constraints. The order is either a fill or kill or all or none.

A FOK order is either completely filled on the first try or canceled altogether. Whereas, An AON order, however, requires the order have the complete number of shares specified or none at all. If it is not filled, that is okay. The order is kept on the books to be executed at a later time.

Day Orders

A day order is the most common type of limit order. This order is only in effect from the time it is submitted through the end of the trading day session. Closing time is defined by the market.

A GTC order requires the canceling order be in a specific way and this is indefinite, though your broker may set a certain limit of days.

Immediate or Cancel orders allow for partial fills, but they are to be executed right away or the exchange is to cancel them.

The type of order you have will be the amount of time you will have to execute your order. Knowing the different order types is fundamental to trading successfully.

Stop Orders

A stop order can be less risky. You, as the investor, buy or sell your stock once it has reached a specified amount. If the price of your stock drops, it automatically becomes a market order executed on the next trade,

You can also use this option in the reverse order. You can specify a certain amount and that then triggers the purchase. Not letting a good deal get away from you!

For example, a buy stop order may be used if you sold stock on a short, with the hopes of the price going down and you then being able to return the borrowed shares at a significantly lower price. This order is used to protect the investor from losses if the prices go too high. It can also be used as an advantage to a declining market.

When you use this option, you want to be aware of price gaps. Sometimes, a stock can close at one price on one day and the next day open at a lower price. While this is not very common, it does happen. Moreover, it will probably hurt. However, don't let that discourage you. The news and media affect the stock prices tremendously. Be patient, and you will bounce back in no time.

Learning the different order types is important and severely underrated in terms of your success. You need to know how these work in order to make the best decision for buying or selling your stocks and when to do it. Stocks isn't rocket science. It just takes a little bit of analytical thinking and strategizing.

Trailing Stop Order

A trailing stop order is a little different from the other orders. This order allows for a stop parameter to be entered. That then creates a moving activation price. This can be entered as a percentage or certain dollar amount of rise or fall in the price of the security. Trailing stop sell orders generally maximize and protect profit.

For example, an investor bought stock with ATT for ten dollars and right away places a trailing stop sell order to sell ATT with a one-dollar tailing stop. That is ten percent of its current price. That sets the stop price to nine dollars. After the order is placed, ATT does not exceed ten dollars and falls to a low price of nine dollars and one cent. The trailing stop order would not be executed because ATT did not fall to one dollar from ten dollars. Later, when the price of the stock rises to a higher amount of fifteen dollars, the stop price resets to thirteen dollars and fifty cents. It then falls to thirteen dollars and fifty cents. That is ten percent of its high of fifteen dollars. The trailing stop sell order is then entered as an actual market order.

Peg Orders

These orders are commonly used in volatile markets. They give the investor the best opportunity possible to get the best price available. These orders are based on the NBBO, which ensures the best offer out there. NBB is the maximum price an investor is willing to pay for a stock. Whereas, NBO is the lowest selling price a trader is willing to accept for their stock.

For example, an investor would like to buy one thousand shares of Company AKM. However, the investor is not willing to pay more than twenty dollars per stock. The current National Best Bid offer is nineteen dollars and eighty cents per share while the National Best Offer is twenty dollars and twenty cents. The investor purchases a peg order with a limit of twenty dollars. When the investor places their order, the market will not see the investors limit price of twenty dollars. It, instead, joins the National Best Bid of nineteen dollars and eighty cents. If the National Bid Offer happens to reach the investors limit price of twenty dollars, an order to buy is then executed.

A mid-price peg order is a little different. Their prices constantly fluctuate and are set at the average of the best bid or offer prices on the market. These orders are usually used on ATSs, where market participants are able to pay half of the bid off without having to reveal his trading intentions to the others beforehand.

OCO

One cancels other orders are for investors whom are looking to only profit from one or two possible trades. Let's say, for example, an investor wants to trade stock TEP for ten dollars or ELP for twenty dollars. In this instance, they would perform a one cancels other order made up of two different parts. A limit order would be issued for TEP for ten dollars and one for ELP for twenty dollars. If TEP's price reaches ten dollars, then the limit order would then be executed. However, the limit order for ELP would be canceled. In order to ensure a disciplined trading routine, OCO's conditions can be automated.

One Sends Other

An OSO order is usually used when a trader wants to send another order but only after one has been completed. In this instance, a trader purchases stock BNM for ten dollars but decides to immediately sell it for ten dollars and five cents to gain the five-cent spread. An OSO order would then be executed in two parts: a limit buy order for BNM at ten dollars and, additionally, a limit sell order for the same BNM stock for ten dollars and five-cents would be created. If BNM stock prices reach ten dollars, then BNM's limit order would be completed, and the sell limit order would then be sent. In other words, several orders are attached to one main order. The orders are then completed in a sequential order.

Tick Sensitive

Upticks are when the last price change is on the up and up. The catch here is the last price can't be zero. A downtick is the exact opposite. It is when the last price of the stock before it changed has gone down. As with an uptick, the last price cannot be zero.

The investor always has the option to use tick-sensitive instruction. To better explain, buy on an uptick. In some markets, short sales can only be completed during an uptick. Subsequently, that makes short sell orders tick-sensitive.

At the Opening

These types of orders can only be completed upon opening the stock market for the day. If this order cannot be executed as the first trade for the day, it is then canceled. Hence, the name, at the opening. These can also be referred to as MOO or Market on Open orders. At no other time of the day can these orders be executed. It is either opening or nothing at all for the day on these order types. These orders are guaranteed, granted if there is enough liquidity.

Let's assume an investor has one thousand shares in Apple. However, they announced a few minutes ago that the sales and earnings will be lower than analysts expected. Stock tends to trade lower in the after hours, and the investor assumes it will continue to do so throughout the following day. They would then execute a market on open order since they believe it will open low and close even lower.

Discretionary Orders

These conditional orders give the brokers the discretion to delay investing until a better price arises and helps improve the order of execution. This allows the investor to have some type of conditional constraints. These are useful for stop-loss orders and limit orders. These can be put into place by a broker or ETS.

For instance, an investor specifies a below market price and also a discretionary amount either through a broker or ETS. If the investor places a buy limit order of twenty dollars on a security priced at twenty-two dollars with a discretionary amount of ten cents, that basically means that they look for stocks priced at twenty dollars but would permit the purchase amount to go from twenty dollars to twenty dollars and ten cents. If the price happens to fall to twenty dollars and ten cents, the order would then be submitted and completed for the investor.

In the case of a discretionary sell limit order, the investor specifies a price above market price for execution. The investor also has to specify a discretionary amount with their order. So, let's say an investor places a sell order at twenty-four dollars on a security that is currently trading at twenty-two dollars with a ten-cent discretionary amount attached to it. The order could then be submitted and executed at a selling price of twenty-three dollars and ninety cents or even higher.

Chapter 4: Let's Get Started

By now, we should understand a good bit about stocks, orders, and how they work. That's only part of the battle of knowledge here! There are a few important rules and guidelines to follow when you begin stock trading. This is a complex topic and should not be taken lightly. When thinking of taking this step, take a long hard thought on your future and that of your family. This chapter is all about you and taking charge of your future self!

Set a Goal

Why are you considering getting into stock trading? Whether it is for retirement or a new home, you must set a financial goal. Take into consideration how much you aim to make from stock trading and the amount of time you want to make said amount. Most people have several different reasons and may need the money from the investments at different times. All these things need to be considered and planned. The longer an investment can stay in place, the greater chance of a return in the positive. Investing for shorter periods tends to be riskier because the value can fluctuate tremendously in a short amount of time. On the other hand, the longer it stretches out, the steadier the value of the investment tends to be.

Setting your goals isn't just limited to the amount of money you hope to make. Your number one goal above all else should be to follow your plan and stick to your budget. This goal alone will take you further than anything. Always be open to new ideas and advice, but unless you can confirm it or afford it, stick to your game plan. No one is going to reach your goals but you, so it's important to be firm with yourself.

Set a Budget

As with anything in life, budgeting is important. Go through your personal finances and see what you can afford to invest. How much would you be willing to lose if things were to go south? Stick within your budget. There is no shame in starting small. Beginning into stock trading can be done with very little money. In fact, a few hundred dollars can usually get you started depending on how you approach stock trading and through what kinds of stocks you invest in.

In the end, don't be scared to take your earnings and go if you don't feel the company stocks will continue to increase. A small return is better than a loss. Taking unnecessary risks can hurt not only your investment but also your bank account as well. However, try to keep the mindset that you are budgeting what you can afford to lose. No, that's not saying you are setting yourself up for failure. That is keeping yourself in a realistic mindset that stocks will not always produce you a profit. You will lose at some point unless you are unbelievably lucky. As I have said before, if it is not within your budget, leave it be. You do not want to start off by getting yourself into trouble financially, even just the slightest debt is too much. Wouldn't you rather want to pay off debt you may currently have or go on a cruise with your friends?

Do Your Research!

Before investing in anything, whether it be stocks, bonds, or even a small business opportunity, it is important to do your research! This is the dirty work of stock trading, but it is necessary. It is not an understatement to say that knowing the company you are looking into investing in is one of the keys to being successful in stock trading.

You want to know the ins and outs of a company, especially paying attention to the customers. The customer base being the most important because you need to see if there is room for growth within that business. For example, if looking at a clothing corporation, you want to know if the business is steady and increasing or if the business is only increasing due to the latest fashion trend. You wouldn't want to invest in something that is only temporary. Knowing the customer base will tell you a lot about the company's ability to grow.

The customer base isn't the only thing that needs to be considered and researched. Researching employees as well is important. Knowing if the executive has the experience and knowledge to run the company as well as the employees that work there. These are the faces and laborers of the company. Their experience and knowledge affect the business and how successful it will be in the end. If the CEO doesn't have a broad knowledge of the company and its products, chances are, the employees are not trained with the proper knowledge either.

Researching a business doesn't necessarily mean that you have to get out and talk to every employee or customer they have. While that may help gather great knowledge and possibly a restraining order, a great place to start is by reviewing the reports a company files with the SEC. They are required by law to file these financial reports, so researching those reports can give one useful and accurate information to start with. Having the most accurate information possible can help you make a well-informed financial investment decision. In fact, many investors and professionals depend on the information found in these filings before and when making an investment decision. Most of the reports can be found online but not all. You can also request the report through the SEC.

We live in a very technologically inclined generation, with the power of the Internet at our fingertips, so researching companies isn't so hard. With that said, most things these days can be found online. Customer reviews are very powerful and can say a lot about a business. It can also show if there is an opportunity for growth and give general ideas of what the company is like as well as it's products. Online forums and, yes, apps like Yelp can give you a sense of the company from the customer's point of view. Without satisfied customers or reviews of poor performance and/or products, you wouldn't want to place that particular company high on the totem pole for your potential investment.

Everything can be found online, however, trading magazines are also a great resource for researching. Many different types of companies are in trading magazines, even pizza joints! The information found in these magazines can be used to analyze companies. That's not where it stops though; these magazines also include different global news about the stock market as well as tips and advice on trading from the experts. Depending on the magazine, there may be different contents included inside. Everything from technology to restaurants can be found amongst the many different magazines to choose from, and it just depends on what you are looking for! These resources have survived the Internet's take over, and it never hurts to have them coming in rotation by the week! The more you know, the better off you are.

Research may be very time consuming and, yes, so is the dirty work, but you want to know all you can about what you are putting your money into and who you are trusting it with. Investing in technology when you are more of a book guy can be a bad idea if done blindly. While it's advised to start with what you know. If you must be a badass and go for the gusto, then make sure that you do your homework. Otherwise, you may find yourself buying and selling for way more or less than what a stock is worth. Knowing the product will help you know and understand the supply and demand and, ultimately, the price. Now, moving forward, you wouldn't trust a well-known thief to hold your paycheck for you while you go for a run, would you? Probably not because you

KNOW that he is a thief. Same applies on the principle that you would want to know who is holding and investing your money on your behalf. Researching literally everything is a must!

Decide on the Right Broker for You

As we have already established, researching isn't limited to just the companies you potentially invest in. The broker company you go with also needs to be researched. As a new investor, some brokers may try to take advantage of the fact you may not know what you're doing. That can cost you more money in the long run.

Back in the day, only wealthy people could afford a broker. Today, we try to make sure that everyone can access things, including brokers. It is only fair that everyone has a chance at the action! Not to mention, prices of things today keep most people on a budget. Discount brokers are a good option. It's like the big coupon you anxiously await to come in the paper once a month! They are able to take on and execute any trade, no matter the type. They only charge a reduced commission fee, usually ranging anywhere from five dollars to fifteen dollars per trade. They are normally paid on a salary rather than a commission. However, they usually don't advise you on investments. Most have a platform for trading online that attracts a number of self-directed investors.

You want to pick a broker that makes beginning easier for you and helps you. Starting with a full-service broker is advisable due to the expert advice that comes along with them. Once again, the more resources you have and the more you know, the better! However, full-service brokers are a bit more expensive. It's important to investigate the fees they charge. Picking a broker that charges low fees or no commission cost and advises you is rather ideal but not very likely. Just like everything good in life, it comes at a price!

Try to find a broker that offers little to no commission costs with mutual fund investments. That is recommended to be one of the best ways to get started into stock trading, as mutual funds are not limited to one stock but split over several different ones. Versatility at it's best! Not to mention, the broker can help you build your portfolio to be diversified.

Overall, your broker decision will ultimately determine the types of investments you will have access to and how much your return will be. The fees they charge add up over time and can add up to thousands of dollars, so it is important to research several different brokers and decide what is best for you and your finances. Don't forget to keep in mind what kind of stock you are wanting to invest in when deciding on a broker. If you are not very knowledgeable about the company, please consider using a full-service broker. It may be a bit more expensive, but they can advise you on what the better move would be. Brokers are there to help you reach your goals.

Choose a Safer Stock to Begin With

Maybe starting with mutual-funds is an ideal way for beginners, but that is not the only option to get your feet wet. As discussed before, focusing on one company can turn into a tragedy if you don't choose a "safer" option. A safer stock would be considered something that, even when everything else is on the decline, people will still need. These are low-risk but they result in lower profits as well.

The type of industry you choose for your stock is important. Things such as food, medicines, and supplies will always be needed, even if the economy crashes. The point of a safer stock option is to have something that is always in demand. How a business pulls through a financial crisis is important. During an economic crisis, you wouldn't expect fast food to have more profit over a grocery chain or a medical supply corporation.

A company's debt is to be considered when looking into any type of purchase. It is certainly not limited to consideration when purchasing or investing into a business. You also need to consider that when purchasing stock. A safe option would certainly not be to invest in a company that has a low enterprise value. Many things affect the enterprise value, but mostly, it is the market cap. In other words, if the stock prices decrease, that affects the overall value of a company more because debt is technically fixed, and cash is just a small portion. Breaking it down a little further, a company owes what they owe to their creditor; the cash they have on hand at the time won't make much difference, but if the investors lose hope in the company and its potential, the loss mainly comes from the stock prices decrease. It's crazy to think that the stock market has that much power over a business, but what's even crazier but somewhat nice to know is that, as a customer, we matter to a company. Not just in the aspect of money but public opinion has a lot to do with the stock market. Indirectly, our opinions as customers are heard in some way other than through rants and raves.

While some may say that size doesn't matter, when choosing a safer stock option, size matters. Well, at least, it's very relevant to consider. Small companies have more room for growth. However, mid- to larger-sized companies have a bigger revenue and a bigger distribution network as well as more experience compared to smaller companies. The chances of failure for smaller companies are greater due to being limited in some areas. Look into smaller companies a little further and be sure to understand the supply and demand of that company and the potential threats to such. Mom and Pop shops are not really a safer option as opposed to Nike. We all know that Nike has a much bigger platform for revenue than a local store owned by the nice old lady and her family down the street.

Putting it all together here, safer stocks are smaller, but, in the end, they are more stable and have a less likely chance of a loss for the investor. When beginning in stock trading, if you don't have the means to invest in mutual funds or just want to get your feet wet a little at the time, safe stocks are always a "safer" option.

However, you choose to invest in stock trading, setting a goal, following a budget, doing your research, deciding on the right broker, and choosing the safer stock can get you started on the right path to being a successful stock trader. In the next chapter, we will discuss the different types of trading and help you decide which type you want to be.

Chapter 5: What Kind of Trader Do I Want To Be?

By now, you should have an idea of how to get started and have your goals set. Depending on what your goals are, whether they are long-term or short-term, there is a place for you in the stock market. Remember, from Chapter 2, when we discussed going through your personal finances and decided what you can invest? This is important in deciding what type of trader you want to be. In this chapter, we will review different types of trading and what each means.

Day Trader

While this is not the trade advisable for beginners, this is a fast-paced buying and selling of stock. A day trader buys and sells stock in one day. All trades are closed by the time the market closes for the day. They start all over again the next day. Day traders have slightly different methods that they follow as opposed to the other traders. They tend to rely on patterns, price differences, and trends to make quick decisions. Let's go over a few examples to give you a better idea.

For example, one method is called Momentum Day Trading. When using this method, day traders simply make a trade while the stock on the market is on a trending movement. At the end of the day, the trade is closed.

Another example is the method Pattern Trading, in which there are instances where stock prices tend to make a diagram or a pattern that becomes recognizable over time. The movements help traders to technically analyze the market and make a sound and usually profitable decision. At the end of the day, this trade is closed as well.

Short-Term Trader

This is the type of trader that holds their stock anywhere from a day to a just a few weeks. This involves a lot of risk as the stock market can go up and down very quickly. Small investors are not advised to do short-term trading or, at the very least, limit it due to the risk of loss. A few weeks can be either show to be profitable or can be detrimental to stock prices and its investors.

These types of traders tend to follow a few of the same methods of trading as the day traders, relying mainly on recognizable patterns and trends and analyzing mathematically when to buy and sell their stock.

Being mathematically inclined and familiar with the charts and patterns are very important when being a short-term trader. After a while, the patterns begin to become easily recognizable. However, when you are just starting, you may not recognize them as quickly and easily. Not to worry! As if you were working out trying to build muscle, repetition makes it easier over time. Not only that but, with time and practice, this will become a no-brainer. Do not hesitate to look over old charts and analyses to practice. That even helps with research in a company as you could begin to notice trends.

Medium-Term Trader

A medium-term trade is the period of trade anywhere from a few weeks to a few months. While this has risks just as short-term trading, it allows for a little more time for the stock market to fluctuate. However, as we have already learned, this could go either way. The Elliot wave trading method is the popular trading method that medium-term traders use. This is a theory based on the thought that the markets fluctuate based on public opinion and emotion rather than news. This suggests that between consumer's feelings of optimism and feelings of pessimism, "waves" are created. It seems that, when bad news is released, the market tends to go up. On the contrary, when good news is released, the market tends to go down. It's basically the psychology behind the stock market trading world. When analysis of the Elliot wave is performed correctly, it can tell you a lot of what the stock market can and cannot do.

Long-Term Trader

Long-term trading is what is recommended for everyone, especially beginners. The reason being, as we discussed earlier, the longer an investment can sit in place, the better off you usually fare. As the name suggests, this type of trading can hold stock anywhere from a few months to years. Returns here usually gain from the growth of the company, bonuses, and such.

An example of long-term trading would be the buy-and-hold method. This method is based on the fact that the world is constantly growing and evolving. When you take a step back and think about it and do the research, you will see that, in the long run, markets have generally good returns. Even despite going through ups and downs, the world still moves forward and continues to grow. Holding onto your stock for longer periods give you a better chance at a positive return.

If you are having a hard time deciding on what type of trade you need to make for what investment, talking to a broker is the best option. Once again, they can be pricey, but you don't want to get started on the wrong track. That could cost you years and more money instead of you being able to enjoy your investment when you aim to have it. This is the key to being able to achieve your goals, especially your long-term goals to send the kids to college or travel the world after retirement. If invested and traded correctly, even if you are only a student right now, you could set yourself up to have all of those things one day.

Chapter 6: Getting Started With Less Money

After going through your finances, you may think that you can't afford to invest in stocks. That couldn't be further from the truth. The facts are, you don't have to be a millionaire to get started into stock trading. That may have been the case a long time ago, but not today! Following a few basic steps can help you get started with very little money. However, we must keep in mind what we have already discussed and learned in the previous chapters. You should already have your goal set and an idea of how long you need to make your goal. Now, let's jump into the fun part and pull both basics together to make you into the best beginning trader on a budget!

Use Your Employer

Most employers offer a 401(k) plan. If you want to get started investing with very little to no money to get started, this is a great way to get you going. Some employers will even match the amount of money you put in. Hey, you bust your butt all week for them, right? Let them thank you a little! For example, if you contribute twenty dollars per paycheck to your 401(k), then your employer may also put in twenty dollars per period as well. That is basically free money! Thanks to the company that signs your paychecks for a little appreciation! Each plan is different, but let's go over what a 401(k) plan is.

A 401(k) is a savings plan for your retirement. With this, you are in control of how your money is invested. Most plans offer money market investments, stocks, and bonds. When setting up your plan, you want to make sure to budget how much you want to contribute, which usually can be set up to automatically draft from your paycheck. Some employers will make you wait for a while before they enroll you, but most automatically do.

There are two different types of 401(k) plans. Both have different rules and conditions to how your money is taxed and how you can access it. The most popular being a traditional plan. The traditional plan allows you to have your money be contributed before taxes are taken out. So, whatever your gross pay is, this is where the amount of your contribution comes from, then taxes are taken out. In other words, the amount of income that is taxable drops because of your contribution to your plan. However, you pay taxes on your earnings upon withdrawal. No, you can't escape paying taxes on it altogether. While you can withdraw early, you would have to pay a whopping ten percent penalty fee as well as the taxes on it. To avoid fees, the rule is that you can't dip into your account before age 59. A small sidebar to that is, if you leave your employer after the age of 55, you won't pay a fee. I guess if you make it that long though, you might as well finish it out and retire with that same employer!

Roth 401(k) plans allow for more flexibility in accessing your money; you can access it if you have had the account for at least five years. While you can access earlier with these accounts, the money you contribute from your check every week comes out after you have been taxed. Resulting in less pay and possibly less of a contribution. On the upside, you do not have to pay taxes when you make your withdrawal. After all, you were taxed pre-deposit, so there is no need to be taxed again.

Even if the company gets on shaky ground and goes under, don't stress! By law, your 401(k) plan is off limits! Most likely, the plan would be terminated, but you wouldn't lose your investment. However, you would have to pay the ten percent fee and taxes. I would much rather pay the ten percent fee than lose the investment altogether. Paying taxes doesn't even seem so bad since you have the added sense of security, knowing that your money is protected.

Consider Using a Robo-Advisor

A robo-advisor is an automated, cheaper alternative to investing your money. It's a digital platform that will ensure that your goals are being met and your investments are doing as they should be. Generally, they have no minimum amount required to get started, allowing you to contribute as little as ten dollars at a time and are cheaper than your typical broker. They give you the freedom to get started without the worry of breaking the bank. Consider using one to avoid paying too much in fees. Everything seems to be going digital, so why not?

Look for No-Load Mutual Funds

There are no-fee mutual funds out there, and you just have to look for them. There are many that offer you to invest for as little as a penny and allow you to make additional purchases at whatever price you would like. Luckily, many of these can be bought and sold without any fee. Hence, the term no-fee. However, you invest in these with the notion that you will need to leave them for a certain amount of time. After a certain amount of time, which is usually five years, you will be able to redeem them with no fees. You need to be careful though, as your broker may charge you fees for stocks bought and redeemed through third parties, and they usually carry fees if you redeem them early. If you are looking to invest for a longer time period, then there is no need to worry.

Consider Investing Apps

While you can go online or through a brokerage company, there are apps that allow you to make investments. These apps use a passive investing model. When making a purchase from a linked source, the app will "round-up" your purchase to the nearest dollar and invest it into your account. You can choose to even triple these round-ups. For example, if you spend $15.75 at the grocery store, the app will take the remaining twenty-five cents and invest it into your account. However, if you choose to triple the round-up, that will be twenty-five cents times three, with a result of seventy-five cents total going into your investment. Try looking into apps like Acorns. They look over and manage your investments while only charging a small fee every month. If you are a student, they will even waive that fee for you! See? There is a place for anyone in the stock world, even students. This makes it almost as though you never even miss the money you are investing from your pocket. A few cents may not seem like much at the time, however, in the end, they add up. This is similar to a savings account feature most banks have. You don't realize how fast it adds up!

Commission-Free Platforms

There are platforms that are online and apps that allow you to buy and trade shares without a commission. They do not have expensive mortar stores, so they are able to do away with the commission fee. The only catch to these platforms is you must have all the money up front when purchasing. On the upside to this, though, is that they have many different stocks and exchange-traded funds for as little as twenty dollars. Hello, budgeting!

Check With Your Bank

While purchasing a certificate of deposit at your bank may not be the most exciting investment purchase you can make, the risks are very low. However, your money will not build fast, but once again, you have basically a risk-free investment. These investments are best left alone as the interest that accrues on it is how you will make your earnings. The catch here is that you have to lock your money up into an account for a certain specified amount of time. It is possible to withdraw early, but you will have to pay a penalty fee.

Granted, if you leave your CD until the maturity date, you will have several different options from there. Your bank will notify you and you can decide to invest in another CD or have your funds transferred to your checking or savings account. If you do nothing, usually, the bank puts it into another CD with the same maturity time frame. However, the interest rates may not be the same. You could get lower rates or higher rates, and it just depends at the time. There is no guarantee that you will receive the same or higher rates. There are several different CD options to chose from as well.

Liquid CDs give you more flexibility. You are allowed usually to pull your cash out at any time with no penalty fee. However, sometimes, you can be limited as to when and how much. That may sound great, but it comes at somewhat of a price, lower interest rates.

Bump-up gives you the option to keep your existing account but go up to a higher interest rate when available. You would need to check with your bank to use your bump-up option. Use them wisely as you do not get an unlimited amount. A lot like the liquid certificate of deposit accounts, these start out paying lower interest rates compared to standard CDs.

Brokered CDs are another option. Instead of going through a bank, you would purchase these CDs through a brokerage account. The idea is that you buy them and agree to leave your money in for a specified amount of time and the bank pays you a certain amount of interest. This is a lot like standard CDs. These give you more of a variety, per se. Because a broker scans and looks for the best rates, you can be exposed to several different banks at different locations, giving you more opportunity. However, these are not recommended for starting traders as it usually comes with a hefty minimum order size. If this is something you truly want to invest in but don't have the minimum, start a savings account to help you build your funds up enough to invest. You will be glad that you did. However, try to avoid dipping into your savings if you hit a rough patch.

Online Brokers

Many online brokerage firms allow you to open accounts and begin investing with a thousand dollars or less. This may come as a surprise, but places like Charles Schwab require a thousand dollars to open an account but can waive that for you if you set up monthly direct deposits of one hundred dollars. Most people use direct deposit for their paychecks anyway, so why not in an investment for your future at the broken-down low price of just twenty-five dollars a week?

Treasury Securities

There are several different types of bonds issued by the United States government. They come in various maturity lengths and have the lowest interest rates compared to the other bonds. You can begin investing in increments of one hundred dollars. These can be purchased through your bank, broker, or through their website.

A treasury bill is a security that matures within a few days up to a year. These are non-interest bearing. Meanwhile, if you purchase a Treasury Note, they have maturity dates of two to ten years, and interest is paid twice a year. Treasury bonds are long-term, with thirty-year maturity lengths. They are fixed principle securities, and interest is paid twice a year once the bond matures. All of these are subject to federal taxes but are exempt from your local and state taxes.

There are plenty of ways to get started without investing a lot of money to start with. You just have to do the research into your finances and consider your goals to put your stock trading knowledge into action! Knowledge, understanding, and patience are the real keys behind any success story.

Chapter 7: Putting It All Together

Okay! Now, we are ready to start putting these plans together and into action! You should now be confident in yourself enough to get your feet wet or, at least, just a little. As you may have noticed, both getting started into stock and doing it with little money are relatively alike. However, it is how you pull the two together that will hopefully ensure your success at being a beginning stock trader.

As we know, setting a goal is the important first step to getting started. How much is the house you are wanting to buy? By when do you want to have this house? Oh, you need to pay for your kids' college too? Okay! Let's write down those goals! It is important to keep in mind that the longer a stock can stay in place, the less risk and more profitable they usually are. As you are setting your goal, by this time you should be able to distinguish what kind of trader you want to be. For different goals, you may need to be a few different types of trader.

For example, if you are thinking about your retirement years, which it is never too early, check with your employer about enrolling into a 401(k). That will get you started. Being able to commit a certain percentage from your check automatically can make it easier, and you can determine how much you want to put, even if it is just one percent of your earnings. That may not seem like much, but when you are on a budget, it definitely adds up over the course of time.

If thinking of buying a house or paying for your kids' college, think longer-term investing. As we have learned, longer investments tend to be more stable and usually have higher returns. Think about the terms of investing into a no-load mutual fund. With a no-load fund, it has no commission fees. Fees add up, and when on a budget, especially for beginners unfamiliar with the market, it can be more than it is worth. If that proves to be something that you are not interested in right now, consider going through a robo-advisor for investing with lower fees.

Researching is not just limited to what broker you want to use or how much your personal finances can afford to invest and possibly lose. Knowledge of what you are investing into is important! If you don't have any idea about biotechnology, you should not be investing in a biotech fund. You need to understand what it is that you are buying, the company behind the product. You also need to understand the supply and demand of that company, the ins and the outs, and everything from the CEO's knowledge down to the customer's opinions. In other words, you don't need to have a Ph.D. on the corporation, but you need to know and understand it, like the back of your hand, before you invest. Not knowing is adding more of a risk that is unnecessary and a rookie mistake. Even if investing with a large amount, those unnecessary risks are not worth it, much less if investing with only a little money! Researching really can't be stressed enough! It is a lot of work and consumes a lot of time but in the end, you will be glad you did!

Whether you decide to go with a broker or buy a Treasury Security from the United States government, stick within your planned budget. As we discussed earlier, some brokers may try to take advantage of the fact that you are new to the game. This could end up costing you a lot of money in fees. Don't be scared to ask around for prices and decline if they are a little too high for you. There is nothing wrong with staying within your means. Go ahead and do some shopping around in the app store and online too. Be firm, even with yourself. After all, you want to be able to invest, live your everyday life, and still buy that house and pay for college later without worrying about how to make it to the next paycheck.

While this may go along with research too, choose a safer stock. Don't just jump in on the advice of a friend. If the numbers are not there to show you from a mathematical analysis that a company has growth and potential, then it wouldn't be considered a safer stock. Other than your own research, talk with your broker if you enlisted one or a financial advisor before you decide. They are experts on the matter and can break it down for you further if needed. This will help you avoid unnecessary risks and give you a better chance of a positive return.

If you are wanting to start with a slightly larger investment but don't have the amount yet, do not be hesitant to do the good ole' cookie jar approach. There is nothing wrong with putting a little money back every week to save up before investing. This would not only give you a larger amount but also more opportunities to buy more investments.

Try to avoid buying on a margin. This is when you basically borrow the money to buy your stock. This is taking out a loan with your broker, and as with any loan, there are hefty fees. You would additionally need to open a margin account with your broker and that usually comes with a minimum investment amount of at least two thousand dollars. That can get pricey. Obtaining a new debt before you can get started and pay off old ones or begin reaching your goals is not a good and reasonably priced way to get started.

Learn the moves of the market. Do not make the mistake of blindly making moves. This can be detrimental to your investment and to your bank account if you haven't invested wisely. Talk with a broker or financial advisor about the different moves of the market to find out which would be better for you at the time. As time goes, you will begin to notice patterns and trends and recognize when the time is right to use what order type. This will come as naturally as breathing over time.

Conclusion

Thank you for taking the time to read *Stock Trading for Beginners: How to Start*. Let's hope that you have found the knowledge and tools to make you comfortable enough to start buying and trading in the stock market world! The tools and resources found here should help you successfully set a goal, develop a plan, and help get you on your way to be a successful beginner. Hopefully, with fat, positive returns! Remember, this is not something that you will grasp in one day or even on your first investment or trade. Practice makes perfect, along with patience and understanding on many different levels.

Now, the next step for you is the hardest part: to get out there and start reaching your goals and planning. Go do the foot and finger work of getting those prices and rates! The world is evolving fast and so are the stocks. You don't want to miss your opportunity to get a jump-start on your future. It is never too early to begin setting up for your life later or even have security if something happens and you need emergency funds. Life happens, and you want to be prepared for whatever comes your way.

Being prepared and aware before you get started has proven time and time again to have more of a success rate. It's quite like studying for a test in school. Reading this book is only part of the battle. Now, it is up to you to go out and make it happen! This isn't rocket science, anyone can do this!

The key to stock trading that doesn't get enough credit is patience. Having patience is going to go a long way and prove to be more profitable. Don't rush yourself. Take your time and make sure that you are investing how YOU want to! This is your money and your life, so take charge and build your wealth as you go! Before you know it, you will be a seasoned veteran in no time!

Finally, if you found this book to be of great help and resourceful to you, please leave a review! It is always appreciated!

Description

If you are considering getting into stock trading but are not sure where to begin, then *Stock Trading for Beginners: How to Start* is the book you have been anxiously waiting for! This should be on everyone's shelves, who want to begin investing in stocks!

It does not matter where you live, how much you make, or who you are. There is a place for everyone in the stock markets. All it takes is a little bit of knowledge to get you started with very little money. It is never too early or late to prepare for your future or the future of your children! Having the knowledge to get confidently get started with a basic understanding of how the market works when buying and selling will prove over and over that you too can do this!

On that note, inside, you will find the difference between the different types of stocks. Yes, there are several! You're not alone in the stock market; find out who all is playing ball with you and what they mean to you as the investor. Some of them are put in place to help you make sound decisions. Basic types of moves on the market is a must-know, along with the basic rules guidelines, and resources to setting your financial goals and planning out how to achieve them all in a timely manner.

Deciding what type of stock trader you want to be can be confusing. Inside, we explain and go over the differences between the types of traders and how that will help you become successful. Do you go through every online forum, app, or broker? Don't stress. This book guides you through the different options you have as an investor, even on how you can invest through your employer or even the United States government. However, there are always things that you need to be aware of. The stock market is no exception to that! There are many risks involved, and you need to be aware of what they are and what the potential consequences can be. This will give you a clear understanding of what may or may not be worth investing in, all this while doing it with as little as twenty dollars.

At this point in life, planning and budgeting are everything. The world can be very volatile at times, resulting in mirroring stocks. Things happen all the time unexpectedly, and being prepared and having a backup plan never hurts. Other than that, you may just want to put away something for you to enjoy later in life. Maybe you want to travel when you retire, and that takes money. However, how you chose to use your money is up to you. You and your family will be glad later that you decided to take charge of your financial future and start investing. Now is the time to get started!

www.ingramcontent.com/pod-product-compliance
Lightning Source LLC
Chambersburg PA
CBHW071151220526
45468CB00003B/1023